How to Accomplish Anything in the World

Darius T. Jones

B K Royston Publishing
Jeffersonville IN
www.bkroystonpublishing.com

Copyright 2024

All rights reserved. This book is protected under the copyright laws. Contents and/or cover may not be reproduced in whole or in part in any form without the express written permission of the author. Brief quotations or occasional page copying for personal or group study is encouraged.

Cover Design by: Elite Cover Designs

ISBN: 978-1-963136-16-6
LCCN: 2024912033

Printed in the United States of America

Dedication

I would like to dedicate this book to my daughter Love Paraway. Daddy loves you more than words could ever explain.

Acknowledgement

My deepest thanks are to those who had my back during times of need.

Thanks to my publisher Julia Royston at "BK Royston Publishing" you have been extremely patient and helpful in guiding me through the whole book publishing process very easy. You and your team remind me every step of the way! You truly change lives and make dreams come together.

I want to give thanks to Kelly and Tara Free Minds Book club, located in Washington D.C you mentor, train, volunteer and guide in any way possible the youth writing workshop. I'm proud to be a member. You were a huge inspiration in how I've been cultivating my mind since I met you. You do wonderful work with the youth and community. You two have such a kind heart. I really appreciate you and the Free Minds Family for their hard work as well.

Dayquan Wright A.K.A Cowgirl I love you so much. I learned a lot from you. You've always told me that I was a master mind and encouraged me to be the best I can be at whatever I put my mind to. You have my back every step of the way. Don't forget friends first and "number one asset."

My son Kareem, I love you

And last but not the least, my mother Vicki Jones who was the first woman, entrepreneur I ever met. You believed in me my whole life and who was also the major factor in the completion of this book. You were sleeping late, waking up early to read over the book, help edit and type up the manuscript while also continuously to give me advice, without you none of this will be possible, so thanks again. You changed my life in so many ways and throughout this book I hope that the knowledge between these pages will remain for generations to come, with that thanks Mom. I love you!

And to the reader of this book, this will teach to play the cards you were dealt but remember to reshuffle, re-deal and play by the cards that you deal yourself and were your choice.

Table of Contents

Dedication	iii
Acknowledgements	v
Introduction	xi
What's an Asset vs. a Liability?	1
90% vs. 10%	5
Prayer Preparation Prevents Poor Performance	7
Different Types of Incomes	10
Knowing a Person's Mind State	13
Smoke Screens	16
Networking	18
Rules of Negotiation	20
All Times Are Not Alike	25
Applying What You're Learned	27

Learning from a Successful Person	29
Knowing Your Type	31
Two of a Kind	34
The #1 Law of Man	40
Self-Education vs. Certification	44
Choices	48
Life on the Road	51
Knowing the Value of One's Life	62
Mirror Effect	65
Politics	67
Staying Ready	72
Paying Attention to Patterns	74
Keep Your Head on the Swivel	76
How to Tell if Your Lover Is Cheating on You	78

How to Tell if Someone Doesn't Like You	85
Get Someone Mad	88
Solutions to Problems That Teens Face Every Day	89
Teen Parenting	90
Cyber Bullying	92
Bullying	94
Product of Environment	96
Dad Was Not There	99
Saying "No" to Drugs	101
What Happens in Relationships, Stays in Relationships	105
Sunken Cost Effect	107
Good Debt vs. Bad Debt	110
How Children Can Earn Passive Income Streams	112
Cash Flow	118

Magic Bounce	120
How Vice Can Easily Get Out of Control	123
How Fast Money Ends Up Slow Money	125
How Getting Locked Up Affects Relationships	128
Does the End Justify the Means?	130
Resource List of Inspirational Books	137

Introduction

Life, what's life? For some, life can mean to live. In this thing called "life," you live and you learn, but wait a minute. When it comes to learning, no person on earth learns the same way or at the same pace. The reason for this happening may very well be dated back to when we were children. The way we learn and what we learn most of the times starts with our parents or the homes we grew up in, with most likely this being the learning process for kids called "indoctrination." For most people, their belief system begins to form early on in childhood. So, you can pretty much already start to see how important certain influences would have on a child's mind early on in his or her development stages while growing into adulthood. When you're a child, you know and understand things by how you were taught. This doesn't mean the things that you were taught were 100% accurate. Although the things you learned weren't 100% percent accurate, it doesn't mean your parents or whoever taught you were bad people or meant to teach you the wrong things on purpose. It just means that at some point in your life here on earth you were misinformed as you were growing up. Even though the people who misinformed you meant well by having good intentions doesn't mean the information they were teaching you were true. As a child, you depend on the people in your life; most of the time adults or the people you look up to can be trusted to help you along the way and lead you in the right direction. As you grow up and start to branch out on your own and explore the world, you will begin to gain firsthand knowledge through your personal experiences and dealings with people from all walks of life. By exploring this book, you shall become more and more financially suave and independent. Your status and mentality shall elevate to a whole new level as you learn to obtain — then apply — 360 degrees of all-around knowledge to performing psychological strategies pertaining to maneuvering and interacting with individuals from any social circle, while living a safe, healthy, long, and prosperous life, only then to eventually leave this world satisfied and adamant about the fact that you, without a doubt, efficiency cultivated the mentality of your offspring, as well as the next generations offspring to come. Not only do you leave a good legacy but you may be saving someone else's life that could be squandering their life and risking their legacy. Better yet, you're leaving a prolific doctrine that's deep rooted and imbedded in the mind of future generations so that they will survive and thrive while acquiring wealth that they, too, may then be able to pass on from generation to generation.

> You have to learn the rules of the game. And then you have play better than anyone else.
> Albert Einstein

What's an Asset vs. a Liability

Does anyone know what an asset is? If not, then it's OK. Let me tell you. An asset adds value and quality to a person's life by uplifting it. A liability is the opposite of an asset. A liability costs money to come out of a person's pocket. Asset are things such as passive income, portfolio, business, vending, landscaping, tow trucks, buying and selling on Amazon. Assets produce and put money into a person's pocket. Assets come in many forms such as people, place, and things. There are some people that may come into your life and add more value to it in various ways. There are places a person might attain to also add value to your life such as job, school, gym, doctor's office, bank or religious assemble, etc. There are places you can go to that will take value away from your life or that may cost your life, such as bad neighborhoods with high crime and drugs. These places will put your life in jeopardy. There are people who may cost you things such as your time, freedom, your energy, or your life. So, remain aware of the counterproductive traits that are associated with liabilities. If something's not holding you down, then it's holding you up. If something or someone creates difficulty for you achieving your goals or success, it's a liability. Cut them off and be productive; the speaking of time, time is one of your most important assets. When you realize you have time to spare is when you should study and read the things that can assist and improve the value and quality of your life and the people around you live that you love. Use your time wisely. Also, always reminder be mindful that your income must outweigh your expense. This is how wealth is created. A person shall never spend as much as they earn. Make sure to keep an observant eye and analytical mind when it comes down to financing any consumer goods, whether it is car, house, clothes, etc. Because when you borrow on interest from others, you become a slave working for others, paying interest to others on borrowed money or purchase. The mind is one of the greatest assets a person may ever have. Most things that materialize on earth first manifest in the subconscious mind. The mind is the one tool that can't ever be sharpened to its maximum capacity. As the mind gets sharper, fewer and fewer premature conversations and vocabulary will form on a person's tongue; meaningless thoughts and actions will become a thing of the past.

The fruit of life fall into the hands of those who will climb the tree and pick them. - Earl Tuffer

90% vs. 10%

When you know better, you do better — or should I say you *can* do better. Knowledge is power once applied in the proper manner. They say a smart man learns from his mistakes, but a wise man learns from others' mistakes. A smart man knows how to get others to do his work for him and always takes credit for the completed work. Make your actions appear to be effortless and practice making them effortless. A great way to achieve this would be to use more critical thinking, strategy, and less physical energy and effort to accomplish the same goal by ultimately working smarter, not harder. The main idea is simply do 10% of the work and gain 90% percent results. Win only and always be about action not just your words.

What we think, we become. - Buddha

Proper Preparation Prevents Poor Performance

Many times, in life, when a person properly prepares for a situation, their performance on that matter increases their chances/odds of successful results. By completing a background check and doing your homework on a matter, a favorable outcome shall be more anticipated than that of a less favorable, undesirable, or unexpected conclusion. Enlighten yourself on different subjects so that you can never get caught off guard. Hope for the best when you succeed at making the proper preparations and expected less or little to nothing when no preparation was executed. When it comes down to emergencies, the same applies. Preparing for a raining day is always a plus or win/ win. You will never know when something bad will pop up out of the blue! It's good to prepare for a rainy day by being financially secure. Having emergency money on hand or stand-by is a great habit to start practicing if you haven't already been stacking or saving your money. Saving money is good but making money is better. While money is not everything, it sure is used for everything. Let's take the board game "MONOPOLY." The first things a person learns quickly is to hurry up and get all three greenhouses; after this, they should then trade the green houses for three red hotels. The point of this switch is whoever lands on the hotels has to pay much more than they would if they were to land on the houses. The primary goal is simple: to spend and use your time and effort acquiring more and more passive income streams.

> Pain is temporary quitting last forever.
> Lance Armstrong

Different Types of Income

The different types of income streams consist of earned income, passive income, and portfolio income. Learning how each income stream works may be very important when it comes to a person's financial success and livelihood. Earned income is the income category in which most people work on or around the clock for money; the earned income stream is usually in the form of an hourly wage. In the earned category the government also taxes us the most. Our next runner-up — and I use the term "runner-up" because this passive income stream consists of money that's still moving while you're sleeping — so whether a person gets up in the morning to go to work or not, money will still be passing through a person's mailbox or banking account. Landlords receiving payments in the form of rent is a great example of someone who is earning a passive income stream. The government takes out fewer taxes in the passive income category than the earned income. Which now brings us to portfolio income. Portfolio income is like passive income in many ways. Portfolio income consists of stock, bonds, and mutual funds; most people refer to these as "paper assets." The government takes out fewer taxes in the portfolio income category. People earn money various ways. There is no "one size fits all," so a person must continue doing his or her homework when it comes to investing. Besides being prepared financially, being mentally strategic is essential to a person's physical and psychological wellbeing. Having knowledge of mind body and soul is always important.

There are no mistakes, those are opportunities gone wrong. - Darius T. Jones

Knowing a Person's Mind State

Having 360 degrees of all-around knowledge dealing with strategies are also very useful. Knowing a person's mind state is also very important because you know what to say to them and how to say it to them. When you do your background check/ homework on who they are, your primary objective is to identify what state of mind that person is in. By doing this, you will then know and understand how to deal with them or *if* you should deal with them. Some things are not for everybody. You can throw different topics at the person to see how they respond. For example, you might not really care for a person, but you speak to them anyway to see how they react, so you say "hi" to them. You might ask them how they are doing. If they say "fine," it might just be a good sign or chance there is really nothing wrong with them. If they respond by saying, "get out of my face," there just may be something wrong with that person. Checking someone's mind state is the same as checking temperature. Knowing a person's mind frame might help you then be able to understand what makes them who they are and how. By having a simple conversation with an individual, you're presented a chance to identify things about them, such as their past, present, and sometimes their future and direction they're headed in life by the vocabulary they often use. Having knowledge about someone is also always good, because this means they won't know your every move! Some of the people in your life will put you down, especially for the things you're trying to do properly. Different people will be required in your circle as you elevate to different levels.

> Procrastination is an expense that no one can afford. - Darius T. Jones

Smoke Screen

It's never a good thing to have your business on "Front Street." This means everything is not for everybody. Keep people off your trail by never letting them on your trail to begin with. Some people have bad intentions. Let's say, for example, you have multiple social media accounts. Everything you do throughout the day, you post it, and let the world know your every move. You go out to eat: you post it. You go shopping: you post it. You go out of town: you also post that. Overall, there's always someone watching your page from frenemies, family, relatives, employers, and the creepy people that your friends with on social media who sent you the friend request about a year ago that you accepted. But to this day, they only watch you to keep tabs and never comment or like anything. The smart thing to do is to post on your timeline a week later. Because, who wants to come back to a house that was broken into. In the business world, it's a good thing when you could identify what a person is capable of, whether it's good or bad. When you identify what a person's occupational capabilities are, this may lead to your doing business with a person by way of networking.

> If you want just the money, you will never make it, but if you love what you're doing and you always put the customer first. Success will be yours.
> Ray Kroc

Networking

When you network with a person, you find out what they're good at. What can I have this person do for me? Why would it be a good reason for me to use this person? What are the pros and cons of my dealing with this person? After you figure out what role they would play in your life, you should then contemplate whether they add more value to your life by being an asset or take value away from your life by being a liability or being a leech and costing you a great deal. Identify who they are, what they know, and their position — yes, I said "position," because life is not always about what you know sometimes it's about who you know that can really make a difference in life. In life, sometimes it takes time for you to know someone before you are able to get through certain doors. This now brings us to a word called "negotiate."

> My mind is the biggest asset. I expect to win every tournament I play. - Tiger Woods.

Rules of Negotiation

When it comes to negotiating, knowing what a person's thinking can be very important! Understanding and having all-around knowledge of the person's mind you're negotiating with can be very beneficial. Let's say for, example, that you're selling a car to a person you know is cheap. The person knows they really need this car to get back and forth to work. You ask for $5,000 for the car. It's 2:00 p.m. and you both must be at work at 2:30 p.m. The man knows he really needs the car to get to work, but he is really being cheap. You tell him that you will work with him and bring the price down a bit by

$1,000. The time is fast approaching 2:15 p.m., and you have15 minutes until you have to be at work at 2:30 p.m. The both of you agree to the cheap man buying the car for $4,000. You leave from where you are and head straight to work. You get to your job 10 minutes late, and now it's 2:40 p.m., so your manager gave you a warning. You sold the car to the cheap man and now he's calling to buy another car the next for his wife. You tell him "no" this time, but he doesn't understand why on earth you are acting mean like this to him. The man tries to explain to you that he paid the full amount to you the last time, but what the man don't understand is that time is not money and that the man selling the car can get compensated back for the difference on the $8,000 car that was sold for $4,000 by selling the next car for straight $8,000 so the next time he wouldn't waste time haggling over the price. The man who brought the car for $4,000 might have come out on top when he brought the car for what he felt was a low price, but look what happened when he tried to buy another car so his wife can have one as well. The car salesman didn't ever want to do business or see him again. Even though he came out on top the first time, the man buying the car burnt what could have been a bridge built to do more business over and over in the future. If you are selling something, start as high or possible then work your way down. Example: Let's say you are selling a shirt. You only want $300 for the shirt, so you start by telling the person you are selling the shirt to that you want $500 for the shirt. By the time the person buying the shirt talks you down, the two of you will probably agree to meet in the middle somewhere around $400 to $450. You only really wanted $300 in the first place. Whether you get $400 or $450, you still win. Sometimes it's not always good to low ball people in a transaction because you might run them away or stop them from wanting to have any future dealings with you. Some people burn bridges with you some or burn bridges before they can even be built. A good business deal is when both parties and sides leave the last transaction feeling satisfied. You won't be able to satisfy everyone. In a negotiation, whoever has the leverage has a better position of power. If you have something the other person wants, you have what some might call a "bargaining chip." The faster you identify your bargaining chip, the quicker you may begin to understand how much leverage you have over a person. The more leverage you have, the more of an upper hand you have. Never bring to the table or deal less than what you said because then you will lose leverage.

Persistent people begin their success whereas others end in failure.
Edwards Eggleston

All Times Are Not Alike

When it comes to time, no times are alike. There is a time and place for everything and everything you do. There is also a time and place for the things that come out of your mouth. Not doing your homework on a matter may lead to problems. Think before you act, and rethink before you react. Many times, in life there are no second chances; that's why you evaluate the whole situation before you act upon instinct or emotions. There is a time when to hold them and a time when to fold them. Wait. Be patient if things are not going the way you plan. Don't just mope around; learn to embrace failure and use that opportunity to turn that challenge to a victory.

Always bear in mind that your own resolution to succeed is more important than any another thing. - Abraham Lincoln

Applying What You've Learned

Keeping up with current events, you always need to know what's going on around you. Watching the news, a person shall always know what's going on around them. Whether it's the economy/stock market, global warming, weather, or public safety awareness. Let's say that you must leave the city you're in because a viral pandemic like COVID-19 started to spread in your city. You prepared for this day to come. You apply some of the information you've learned in this book and began to change your primary income from earned income to passive income by understanding what an asset is. You saved your money and bought an apartment building on the street you once rented an apartment on that is an asset. Now you receive rent money instead of living from paycheck to paycheck. Now you no longer must go to work at a job because you learned 90/10 rule and begin working smarter, not harder; you properly prepared for a rainy day by putting emergency money to the side. As you reflect on this book that your mentor referred to you a while back, you understand now how important it is to learn from a successful person.

> What would life be if we had no courage to do attempt anything. - Vincent Van Gough

Learning from Successful Person

They say, "monkey see, monkey do," so watch what you do around people. There are people who are always watching what you are doing. You may also be a person who watches others. This is called "life." There is nothing anyone can do about this. In life, things happen. When things happen, you want the best possible outcome. With this being the case, in life you want to learn from the people who have already done and succeeded at what you're trying to accomplish. If you have not mastered a project or pulled off a certain task, find an expert in that field who knows the specific craft or trade. As your understanding of the world advances, the roles that people, places, things, and positions play may also be better beneficial to you if you first properly prioritize by being able to tell the difference between an entrepreneur, manager, and technician from each other.

> It takes 20 years to build a reputation and five minutes to ruin it. If you think about that you'll do things differently. - Warren Buffett

Knowing Your Type

When it comes to people, places, and things, some things are easier said than done or done than said. The reason saying and doing are two or can be three different things is that you have three different people when it comes to executing and accomplishing a goal, on this list, we have the entrepreneur, manager and the technician. When it comes to being creative, organizing, and operating various business ventures while having a clear finished picture with the end results in mind, is what make an entrepreneur who they are. Entrepreneurs must stay on course, keep the vision of the finished picture and the end results in mind. Having the right management can make or break a project. Let's take fast-food restaurant workers who always have "no call" or "no shows on" the evening shift. On top of this, the manager steals the earnings from that day out of the safe during his shift. To make a long story short, the fast-food store closed because they never met their quota due to the mismanagement of funds! If the management had been taken care of by someone who wasn't a slacking, dishonest thief who didn't just let people call off whenever they wanted, the bottom line would have been met at the store as they succeeded by having the proper management in place. The positions of each technician would have been distributed according to each individual's strength and weakness. Good management not only knows how to assign the right people to their proper positions, but, if need be, they also, to a degree, can do technical work as well. As the saying goes, a good team leader must first understand and know how to be a great follower first. A chain is only as strong or as weak as the weakest link. The same goes for any organization. An organization success or failure depends not only on the leader and the people at the top, but all the way down to the people putting the foot and hands technical work in at the bottom. Without technicians, who would have built the building and made the pages of the book you're now reading these words of wisdom in?

> You miss 100 percent of the shot you don't take
> Wayne Gretzy

Two of a Kind

There are two kinds of people when it comes to a purchase. The two parties that make up the contractual agreement of the negotiated purchase are called the seller and buyer. A price must be paid when a purchase is made. Depending on what you're trying to accomplish through your purchase, the price may vary. There are three different prices when it comes to a sale or a purchase. You have the manufacturer's prices, the wholesale price, and the retail price. The manufacturers produce the finished products on a large scale. Most of the time, the manufacturers sell their finish products in bulk or high quality to the wholesalers. When the wholesalers receive these products in high quantity or volume from the manufacturers, they mark up the price of the products by reselling the products to retail. Retail buys the finished product from wholesalers and mark up their prices as they then resell the goods or products to the consumer. As you retain the knowledge taught to you in this book and apply these principles to your everyday life, you will begin to understand that when a person walks into a store it's two people. I know, I know, you're wondering what I'm talking about when I mention one person walking into the store, but it's two. I meant to say there are two *types* of people when really, there is only one person with two different mindsets when it comes to a price. You have the mind frame of the poor person when they see a price, who says things like, "I can't afford that" or "that costs too much." Now you have the mind frame of a rich person. They say things like "how can I afford that?" The first mindset is the mindset of a person who is not motivated, they don't believe in themselves and never attempted to make things happen. The second person is the person who asks themselves, "how can I afford that?" When they see a price or something they want to purchase, when they ask themselves this question, the wheels start turning in their head on bright ideas and different way to earn money for what they have their eyes on. A great way to earn money is by arbitrage, understanding different markets you approach as you finesse supply and demand prices, so they appreciate as you see your return on investment. The more products that are around, the more price tends to drop. The fewer products, the more likely the price for them will go up. A person will come up with a certain price for their products. Buying for low in one market and selling for high in another is the primary agenda for someone who practices arbitrage. Let's take an online retail company like Amazon. There are people around the world who shop on Alibaba.com searching for manufacturers' prices and wholesale prices, so they can buy in high quantity or bulk just to resell the products on a retail site like Amazon for a mark-up value and make a high profit. To make money on Amazon.com, you sell products. Well, if you are, then you're like millions of others who also have the same question. How do I start selling on

Amazon.com? If you were looking for the answer, look no further. You first contact Amazon, and tell them you want to be a professional seller. They are going to walk you through the whole process, after Amazon sets your account up, you then contact vendors like Alibaba.com for your products at a low price. Then you sell the products on Amazon.com that you have imported from the manufacturers at Alibaba.com. You probably have noticed by now that this book has been formed to enlighten and touch basics on various life-learning experiences and topics dealing with everyday wants and essential needs that you will need to survive life or life during a pandemic or worldwide catastrophic event. This brings us to the "#1 Law of Man or Mankind." Some of you out there may be wondering what in the heck on

Earth I'm talking about now. It's perfectly fine if none of you knows an answer to the question.

> Nothing in this world can take the place if persistence. - Calvin Coolidge

The #1 Law of Man

The #1 Law of Man is self-preservation; you can call it the "#1 Law of Mankind" for those of you who may feel as though I am being politically incorrect. I know that so far in this book we have been covering many important topics. Why there was plenty of knowledge learned early on in this book pertaining to all-around life lessons, which are lessons at the top of the list that have been proven to be vital to one's survival and even one's existence. This brings us to where some might think we should have started in the first place, depending on your background or maybe how you were taught as you were growing up, whether your lessons consist of fact or opinion. No matter who you are on earth, you have perception and you have choices. The difference between the two are understanding. Perception is how a person sees the world. "The glass is halfway full." "No, the glass is halfway empty." This does not mean thinking that the halfway full glass was right or that the halfway empty glass was wrong. This now brings us to choices. We can choose to leave the glass halfway empty, or we can fill it up and keep it that way by using your chance and choice wisely. By taking care of the responsibility of keeping the glass always filled up, we now have the knowledge to understand that by having the glass halfway empty was wrong and not a good thing to let happen. By now exercising our right to choose and applying knowledge that we at first didn't have the intel for or possess the knowledge. As you mature on both plains, mentality and physically in life or before your mind was cultivated and was introduced to this book, you just didn't know. The infancy stage of or person's understanding of life and responsibility for being a provider in their family and home. What exactly is the #1 Law of Man? For some it's providing for oneself first. For you to be able to take care of yourself you need knowledge and education. But wait! What kind of education? This depends on a few things, such as what you're trying to accomplish in life. You may go to school and get good grades, which may lead to getting a good job working for someone else. You may get your high school diploma. In the next chapter, let's talk about self-education vs. certification.

> Success is liking profit, liking what you do, and liking have you don't. - Maye Angelou

Self-Education vs. Certification

There is a difference between education and certification. Anybody can go to a public library to self-educate themselves on a particular subject or matter. Why having an education is very important: a certification is a certified document that pretty much speaks for itself and says this person has the education or experience needed or required for a certain position. Does this mean a person with a certification is smarter or better qualified for the position than the self-educated person who may be much smarter when it comes down to the matter of different jobs and qualifications? Absolutely not. But in the professional job-ready workforce setting, supervisors and employers most of the time are only going by someone's credentials if they truly haven't seen a person's skills. Every situation may vary depending on the person or skills they have. Anyone can without a certification go to a public library and learn how to self-educate themselves. Just having knowledge alone many times just won't cut it. There is a process that is called "application." It's pretty much using information and intelligence to have something done with a person who might have knowledge of how to do something, but never accomplish anything they need done for themselves because they lack action behind their words. Their words will remain exactly just what they are — just words! On the other hand, you have a person who doesn't have much knowledge about a particular subject as the so-called smart person. But they are smart enough to get that person to help them at this point, so these two individuals' IQ will kind of balance out. Both abilities are measured at the same level. Never forget that your mind is your greatest asset, so keep sharpening it. A person with a sharp mind not only knows plenty of things but their actions, also, display these things as well. Move and win through actions, because the moment you start telling the people around you what you have planned and don't go through with it, is the point where people start not to take anything you say seriously. It's good to let people know when you're doing something but when you notice the deadline coming up or that you can't keep up with your promise, stop running your mouth and start getting things done behind the scenes. As you execute the goals on your list one by one from your short-term goals all the way to your long-term goals!

Opportunities are usually disguised as hard work, so most people don't recognize them. - Ann Landers.

Choices

Choices can help us, and they can hurt us, but choices? What are they and how do they affect us? If you don't know, then you're in luck. Think about this morning when you woke up. You had a choice of which outfit you wanted to wear outside today. You also have a choice of who to have as a friend. When you and your friends hang out, you will also be presented with a choice to say "yes" or "no" to things such as using guns and other dangerous and negative things. What if one of your so-called friends one day says to you, "Hey, we all smoked this so now it is your turn to try the drugs." What should you do?

Do you give in because of peer pressure, or do you stand up for yourself and have a mind of your own? You tell your friends "no!" You don't want to smoke. If you don't stand for something, you will fall for any and everything. Just because they're messing up their lungs and life doesn't mean that you must do the same as well. Be a leader of the leaders instead of a follower of the followers. Hand-pick your friends and be careful not to rush because you're the average of every person you hang around. You can pick and choose your friends in life, but you can't pick what family you were born into. With this being the case for many, you must make the best out of that which you have been given until better comes along. Tomorrow is not promised to anyone, so be grateful for who know or what you have. At the same time, consider altering your situation, if you truly don't like the cards you were dealt. Reflect on the knowledge pertaining to enlightening oneself family and friends. To 360° of performing obtaining lessons of financially literacy and psychology strategies while advancing from page to page then to the end of this book. You shall practice increasing your odds/chance to not only play with the hand you were dealt but also to create or adjust to the hand that you did not get.

> A single point of failure (SPOF) is a system that contains only one component to do a job… if that single component fails, there is no alternate one to take its place. - PC Magazine

LIFE ON THE ROAD

Life is like a car traveling on the road. Let's say, for instance, that your car is driving on the highway. There are signs on the side of the road that are warning you to slow down, but you are speeding. There are other signs you pass as you continue speeding. On the left side of the road, you have a sign that is telling you to slow down and proceed with caution: "road work up ahead." Some people may refer to this as an obstacle or mid-life crisis. No matter what it's called, there are other warning signs that say "detour." You have been speeding in your car for so long that when you tried to hit the brakes to slow down, they fail to work as your car then continues to fly past the exit signs. Or should I say *warning* signs that you've failed to pay attention to. Had you paid attention to the signs, you would have noticed the sign that said "warning obstacle" or "road work being done up ahead." But the problem went unattended for so long, you crashed into it. You didn't pay attention to any of the signs, the signs you were messing up in life. The signs are the things your family and friends were telling you every time they pulled up on you to tell you about how you were not living right. All the warning signs that your life was spiraling out of control that you ignored. Yeah, the signs you ignored all the way up until you crashed, right after you had one last time to exit the road you were traveling when you overdosed on drugs, got shot and survived, got locked-up and came home when you were facing a lot time, when you knew the judge could have put you away for life, you never changed your life and exited that road when you had a chance to exit when you saw the exit sign. Your mid-life crisis was an obstacle in your road up ahead. There were warning signs the whole way up to the exit sign you could have taken to change your life, but you were so out of control that you flew past the last exit and crashed right into a wall that was road work and an obstacle in your life because you failed to get help and exit while you had the chance for which ultimately led to your end. Pay attention to your warning signs in life and make sure you're able to identify all your exits long before it time to exit. In life as you began to mature and identify when you have an exit coming up you will be presented with two things and those are a choice and a chance to choose to take the change to change for the good or bad or better or worst. What a person does with their chance to make the right choice is very important; because they may not have an opportunity to make a correct choice.

On the flip side, if you have breath in your body, you have a choice. You take care of your responsibilities in your life and stopped making the same mistakes you had been making before you got your life together. You're able to deal yourself a good hand and play by the hands you deal, because when proper preparations prevent poor performance, many of your outcomes may result in wins, opposed to losses as you increase your odds/chances of much more favorable outcomes. The time will come when will power and self-control is tested on things like when to turn off the path by way of the exit or to which car you wanted to drive, which friends to have and whom to have a family with. You have a chance to make a choice to take a chance of who to lie with. It's simple as this when you make good decisions in life you increase the chances of more choices being available. When you make reckless, unsound choices you risk having the option of being able to make more choices. Put value on the choices you make. For example, let's say that you get off from work every day at the same time. You know a police officer lives on the corner of the street you live on; however, you took a chance and made the choice to go against your best judgment and got drunk, then flew past the officer in your car on the way to your house. In your heart and mind, you knew drinking and driving wasn't a smart idea, but you chose to also speed past the officer's house and attract attention to yourself. Now you're under arrest and therefore lost the option to drive because you behaved recklessly and made the wrong choices, which led to your owning a BMW because your car was taken by the police when they arrested you. That's right: you own a nice BMW because from here on out that's what you have is the Bus Metro or Walking while you still have a chance to make the right choices. That's my definition of a real BMW. The older you get; you should begin to form habits that reframe from stinking or negative thinking and toward more habits of positive thinking. Always keep the bigger picture in mind. Sometimes you must break yourself down to effectively build yourself back up. Periodically do some self-reflecting and re-evaluate your goals to make sure they are still worth obtaining and not a waste of time. You give up on yourself the moment you let go of your discipline. As you start to intentionally plant seeds of important values in your life. Inevitably these things are going to start manifesting in all directions.

The things you have been doing up until this point in life and the things that you are reading in this book, have made you who are. But, by using the new information that you learned at the beginning of this book, your sub-conscience mind shall begin to apply the knowledge from the beginning to the middle, then apply all that information retained in the middle to be used and applied all through to the end.

As you continue through this book and reflect on the lessons in each chapter, it will be completely normal if your mind were to begin wondering how you would act or handle different situations better. Your subconscious mind along with your newly trained eye shall begin to pick up on and identify things much faster than at first. Things like what an asset is, opposed to what looks like and appears to be an asset but is really a liability disguised as an asset. Your financial literacy shall expand as you apply the obtained knowledge you've learned to earn more passive income from various sources, at the same time you should began to comprehend how to properly negotiate business deals. While remaining alert to when to seize the perfect opportunity to network, interact then use strategy to maneuver around people of different positions of power on the highest level or platforms, all the way down to an underestimated pawn of the lowest perceived position of your perceived understanding and magnitude of your mind. Whether you subconsciously place a higher value on someone else life or whether someone else place a lower value on that persons' life, another person or you at the end of the day what matters the most is the value you put on your life. Because no one is going to value your life like how you value your life. So let me be the first to tell you if you haven't heard it before. Congratulations! Give yourself a pat on the back. If you made it up to this point in this book that means you value your life and take it seriously. They say your property is just as valuable as the security you put around it. You even must secure the things on your body. For example: the reason you have a gate around your tongue is because if you don't consider what comes out of your mouth you can get yourself killed and lose your life or if you don't consider what you put in your mouth as toxins you can lose your mind or your life. You also must secure what is between your legs because if you have unprotected sex with the wrong person a deadly disease may take your life as well. If you don't want your life taken from you, secure your property secure yourself in life by not jeopardizing or putting yourself in harm's way. But wait a minute! You're probably thinking that I don't do any risky things. I don't smoke at all; I also eat healthy and I don't do drugs. I mind my business; I meditate. To make a long story short, I live a healthy and productive lifestyle. You live your life how you do and strategically move how you move because you truly value your life. When it comes to the value of another person's life, who's to say what that value is. This brings us to something called "perception." Because no one or two people on earth are alike or have the same life, nor do no two people understand and live the same way. What's the value of life? This brings us back to who has value.

> Good artist copy, great artist steal.
> Attributed to Pablo Picasso

Knowing the Value of One's Life

It's one thing to know the value of your own life, but someone knowing the value someone of else's life is a whole other thing. Sometimes in life people may place the wrong value on someone else's life depending on their motive or perception. Once you began to identify and notice that you aren't being valued or appreciated by someone, that is the moment you're presented a choice. You may first try talking to the person to let them know how you feel about the way they have been mistreating you. After this you can wait to see if they change, if they act better; if they don't, you may act, such as hitting that person and hurting that person and risk getting yourself in trouble with the law. But you're bigger than this, you have self-love and self-esteem for yourself wherein you value yourself to where your reputation is respected by others to the point that if you were to stop showing your face and coming around as much, the value of you would continue to increase more and more as you make yourself less available.

People appreciate things they can't have. Know your worth! People will only treat you how you allow them to treat you. It's pretty much like this: it's not what people call your situation that matters — it's what you respond to that defines you that matters. So, who are you? Really! Who are you when no one else is around? It's not what you do when someone else is looking that counts, it's what a person does when no-one is looking that counts. If you want to see how a person is, do business with them. Sometimes you won't be able to get the chance to do business with a person, but you may still be able to see how they did business or conducted themselves with someone else. They also say a smart man learns from his mistakes, but a wise man learns from others' mistakes.

That's why they say you have two ears opposed to one mouth, so you can listen twice as much as you should speak. Become a wise businessman or woman.

Financial peace isn't the acquisition of staff. It's learning to live on less than you make, so you can give money back and have money to invest. You can't win until you do this. - Dave Ramsey

Mirror Effect

Treat people how they treat you. The same energy someone is giving you, give them right back. If someone treats you well, you treat them well back, or you could decide to treat them great, by going off someone's intentions. If someone treat you badly, it's up to you if you choose to treat them worse. But I don't recommend for you to treat them badly or negatively back because you're now giving this person too much of your energy to begin with. Don't let no one rent space or live in your head for free. You may subconsciously start spending more energy than you should on a person whom you can't benefit from. When you let things go, you more than anything else do yourself the most benefit. Here's why. Not letting things go, you may end up stressing yourself out raising your blood pressure, hair loss, loss of appetite and more. To sum this all up, this person has the character traits as someone who is a liability.

On the other hand, this goes the other way to, as well. Such as if a person is not paying you no attention, that's fine. You simply take your attention away from them. After doing this, sit back and watch how they respond. Human nature is that people want what they can't have. Just keep in mind, do unto others as you would want them done unto you. In this thing called life you reap what you sow. You want to be around people who have the same values as you.

Men acquire a particular quality by constantly a certain way. - Aristotle

POLITICS

What is politics? Not politicians. When I mention politics, I'm talking about people and how a person or situation may affect another are of someone else's life through a word we know as influence. There are many things that may occur on a day to day, a week to week and month to month basis, etc. Some of the events may be completely random as for others not so much. Because at the end of the day or beginning of the night, it really won't dawn on you if you never experience that action taking place or having took place. Some past interferences and influences can affect the things that will happen in the future. Let's say for example: One day you were driving fast down the street to make it to a building where you were scheduled for a 1:30 p.m. appointment. It's 1:25 p.m., and you pulled into the parking lot so fast that you almost hit the man sitting in his car waiting for the parking space you just took. You're in a rush, and you were already mad because you were running late, so you cussed the man out as you were getting out of your car. After locking the doors to your car, you enter the building in a hurry knocking over an old lady in the process and kept on going. You made it to the floor you were scheduled to be on, and the old lady behind the desk smiled at you as you were giving her your name; she then got up and walked to the back to tell her boss that you were there. She then came back out to the waiting room where she was to tell you that there would be at least a five-minute wait, so her boss can come in to do your interview. Time passed. You look at the clock on the wall when suddenly you heard a familiar voice call your name from the room where your interview was to be held. As soon as you looked up so you could go in the direction your name was called, the blood in your face drained. Immediately, it dawned on you that the voice you heard was from the old man you took the parking spot from when you pulled up to the building. To make matters worse, the old lady you bumped on the way into the building was his mother on the way in to bring the interviewer his lunch. She then entered the room and immediately noticed you sitting there. She spoke a few brief words with her son, the interviewer, which you couldn't make out. But because you closely paid attention to patterns and body language, you pretty much knew that the interview was over at that point as the mother and son both smiled as you headed out the office and drove back to your home. That job you were there for was long gone; politics played a role in you not getting the job. One event affected another; had you conducted yourself as if you were being watched from the beginning, you could have gotten the job. Character is who you are when no-one else is around or looking. Had it been the other way around, when you are kind and just gave the man the parking space because he was there waiting for the spot before you or helping the old lady would have been the right thing to do. The people who interviewed you would have seen you as a nice person, which most likely would have resulted in you getting the job. You never know when someone is watching you. So always conduct yourself with morals and principles.

Fortune sides with he who dares. - Virgil

Staying Ready

Learn how to practice and establish good habits. A great habit to start practicing is staying ready, I mean in multiple ways and on various platforms and levels. If there's a war going on and the battle is seconds away from starting, do you think it would be the brightest idea for a solider on either side to start sharpening their weapons or tools at the last minute? If you don't know the answer, it's "No." Once he began to see the other army heading in his or her direction it's too late. Always stay prepared and keep your tools sharp because underestimating a situation, person, place, or thing can be detrimental to you or anyone else like you who didn't educate themselves properly. Staying ready financially is also very important because there are always good investment opportunities that may arise when you least expect it.

> Victory has a thousand fathers, but defeat is an orphan. - John F. Kennedy

Paying Attention to Patterns

Patterns: what are they and why do we need to pay attention to them? As you began to learn how to spot a pattern, there are some very important things that you must identify first, and that's the context clues that either point to the model or surround what we must comprehend as the standard to compare what we understand as the normal or outside the norm, as we gather intel from the origin or model. Let's say that you're on your way home, and you notice that you are being followed. How did you come to this conclusion? Easy! You made it a habit to pay attention to your surroundings, to make sure that nothing was unusual or suspiciously out of place. The goal is to always be aware of your surroundings without being overly paranoid.

There are people who make things happen, there are people who watch things happen, and there are people who wonder what happened. To be successful, you need to be a person who makes things happen. - Jim Lovell

Keeping Your Head on the Swivel

What does it mean to keep your head on the swivel? If you are reading this that means you're probably asking yourself, why should I keep my head on the swivel? Here's why.

Let's say you are walking down the street with both of your headphones in your ears. You can only hear the music playing loudly in your ears, so you fail to hear the gunman a half a block away shooting random people, or let's say that instead of a gunman it's a stray Pitbull with rabies heading in your direction, but you're not paying attention to the people around you trying to get your attention by waving, trying to flag you down. Use your reflection in mirrors, all windows, buildings, cars, water puddles — whatever will arm you at saving your life.

> Action is the foundational key to all success.
> Pablo Picasso

How to Tell for Sure if Your Lover Is Cheating on You

How can you tell if your lover is cheating on you or lying to you in any way? For many people, this bothers them in a relationship, especially if they have been cheated on in a previous relationship. This by itself will cause some serious trust issues. If this doesn't happen, and most of the time it does, this stinking thinking begins to be nothing but baggage. So, the hurt person will probably start off good then as time goes on, then most of the times turn into the problem that previously broke up their last relationship. Why would these become patterns? Also, the person might start cheating in the new relationship just because they have been hurt before already. But this can go two ways. The person may not cheat because they were once cheated on. They know how it feels, so they take steps to make sure that the person that they love doesn't get their heart broken as theirs once was. They might subconsciously become satanic; now they enjoy getting off on inflicting pain. No matter what happened in their previous relationship, what the person needs to do is focus on the relationship that's in front of them. If you and your lover doesn't seem to be working out, it's fine; try couple's therapy and if that doesn't work, walk away while there is not that much time wasted.

When you or your lover leaves the house, sometimes the question may pop up as to where this person is right now. I know your lover told you that they were going to work, but how do you know this to be 100% true? I mean you would sure hope that they told you the truth because why would they lie to you about where they're going? They never gave you a real reason not to trust them. The thought came to you when you were up late one night while your lover was fast asleep. You couldn't help but notice that none of their cell phone notifications were going off as they had been for years. You think to yourself that this is quite strange. You never looked through their phone before because you two always respected each other's boundaries. But neither one of you ever had a locked screen on your phones. You quietly reach over them without waking them up. You succeed, you have more and more questions. This was the fifth time this week that your lover purposely placed their phone face down. So, you picked up the phone; now it has a lock on it and a locked screen with a security pin code to unlock. You try her birthday and the name of the dog that you bought them for Christmas or birthday. None of them work so you put their phone up to their hand, still being quiet making sure you don't wake them up. You're in the phone; their fingerprint unlocked it. You know exactly where to start looking because you read and learned what to do in a situation like this in the book you're now reading. You waste no time. You go right to the home screen, and you look for the google map app. After you find this, you open the app. You go straight to timeline explore and search history. Then you go to the calendar and click a day. It's going to give you that person's entire travel history since they had that email. If that person had their location on, the app is going to give you step by step where this person went, when and how long, where the place was, they went to and time they left the place and whether it was a bus, train, uber, walk, bike, or plane.

I know some people out there may think this is an invasion of privacy. But if you want to really know and find out what the people around you are saying behind your back, it's very easy. Put your phone on video mode and push record. Continue to talk to the mark/intended target and play music so you don't draw attention to yourself. Before you leave the room, your target is in, place your phone or any recording device where it can't be seen by anyone. After planting the device, you then should leave the room for a while to let the person or people you're trying to catch talking about you talk about you. After you wait a nice little while, you then come back in and discreetly recover the listening device you planted prior to leaving the room. You should go somewhere quiet and make sure there is no sound coming from anywhere. You want to make sure you hear everything correctly coming from the recording device. You will be presented with two things, that's a chance to choose what to do after you received the intel on what you heard on the listening device. You could play everything cool and act as if you didn't hear or know anything. On the other hand, you can approach the person about what you've heard. But wait a minute — you know what they did, and they know what they did. So, it's pretty much like at this point, you're now beating a dead horse. What do you do when you find out about what this person has said behind your back? This is very simple. You can cut them off. There is no need to argue with the person. An empty can makes the most noise. What's understood doesn't ever need to be explained. So, watch the company you keep.

Success is dependent on effort. - Sophocles

How to Tell if Someone Does Not Like You

In life some things are not what they seem! You might think that a person is truly your friend, but you don't know for sure. So how do you find out if a person is your real friend? You may find this out the easy or the hard way. Only time will tell the real from the fake. A person may be friends with a person for years before they noticed that the person is not really their friend. But wait, who wants to wait for years later when they are old and gray before they find out that a person is not their real friend. What do you do when you have a problem like this? Easy, you can do a few things. Like put that person through some test. If you have a friend, you are not sure you trust, you put then through test by sending someone else their way to talk bad about you. After doing this, you then wait and see if your friend joins in with the person that you sent to talk bad about you. When you do this, you will want the whole conversation recorded, so you can have proof of what was said for yourself. You most likely should tell the person that you sent to your friend to have a recording device to make sure everything gets reported back correctly. Now this can go two ways. Let's say for example: that your friend really doesn't mess with the person you sent there way or really deal with them so your person/mark whatever they wanted to hear just to get rid of that person, so your friend can come back to tell you what the other person said. This can also go wrong. What if your friend was going to come back and tell you what the person said but forgot. What should you do at this point? What can you do? Well for starters you can give them the benefit of the doubt and wait for a minute and test their motive by bringing up that person's name in a casual conversation. At this point it should have dawned on you that if your friend didn't say nothing and warn you after hearing the mention of that person's name there is a good chance that your friend is not your friend and therefore can't be trusted.

> Success is how high you bounce when you hit bottom. - George S. Patton

Get Someone Mad

Many times, in life if you get someone mad enough, they will tell you how they really feel about you. People often hold their tongues or try to hold their tongues. With a drunk tongue speaks a sober mind, so many times the things a drunk person says out of their mouth or through a text has a lot of truth to it. But wait, the person doesn't have to be intoxicated to speak about how they really feel. If they get mad enough or just fed up, they will tell you how they really feel.

> Start where you are. Use what you have. Do what you can. – Arthur Ashe

Solutions to Problems That Teens Face Every Day

Problems that teens face, for example, teen parenting, cyber-bullying, drug overdose — it is school for me. If not, how do I solve problems for myself? I have parents talk about taking drugs, practicing safe sex, fitting in with the 'in crowd,' how to love yourself, the reason fast money can end up becoming slow money, how to stand up to a bully, avoid becoming a product of your environment and intellect over emotions.

> Alone we can do so little. Together we can do so much. – Helen Keller

Teen Parenting

The reason I mention teen parenting is if you're a teen and become a parent and didn't plan for it, there are things that you must first understand. This goes back to the #1 Law of Man or Woman and the survival concept of self-preservation. The number one concept of this is to basically be able to take care of yourself before you can be able to take care and provide for anybody else. If you can't provide for yourself, how can you take care and provide for another life? But wait, there's more.

Let's say that you can provide for yourself and a child financially. This child also needs nourishment, time, attention, love, soothing, care, morals, values, safety, education, family, a home, and you. The food and clothing, shelter is in the self-preservation category. Keep in mind that a child's mind is like a sponge. Children will repeat and do whatever they see around them; what they see people do, they will do or try to do. Make sure to keep all negative influences away from children. As the child gets older, you will want to teach the child to have morals, values, and principles.

> A diamond is a piece of coal that stuck to the job.
> Michael Larsen

Cyber-bullying

Bullying is one thing, but cyber-bullying is something totally different. We are going to cover bullying in the next chapter. Let's get back to cyber-bullying: what is it? It's when someone bullies someone on-line; most of the time the bullying is done through social media. The topic is very, very serious. Let's say that a young girl around the age of 13 posts a photo of herself on social media, and ten minutes later a few of her negative liability, unethical friends having class comment under the young girl's post by saying "look at those pimples on her face." There are other followers who laugh at and start sending emojis to pick on the girl as well. The young girl was always self-conscious about her face and herself because she never had a role model to show her how to love her skin or herself first, leading her to being at her breaking point that causes her to hang herself one day after school. This can happen to anyone, or anyone's family member, so treat everyone as you will want to be treated. Treat people right when you're young, or bridges will be burnt when you're older.

A dream doesn't become reality through magic; it takes sweat, determination and hard work.
Colin Powell

Bullying

There are different types of bullies. That's right! You have the physical bullying that's pretty much an assault that is done to a person who is getting picked on. Another form of bullying is done verbally, whether through name calling or putting a person down. If by any chance a person were to find themselves in a situation like this, the first thing you do is as soon as it happens the first time, pull the so-called bully to the side and look them in the eyes while letting them know you don't play or mess around like that. If they continue, make them realize you mean business, because running isn't an option. If that doesn't work, be the bigger person and walk away.

If your dream is a big dream, and if you want your life to work on the high level that you say you do, there's no way around doing the work it takes to get you there – Joyce Chapman

Product of Your Environment

Let's talk about how a child or person is raised. There are influences other than a child's home that may play a major role in the child's life as they grow into a teen, then into adulthood. There are positive and negative forces that may have a huge impact on child or teen. Many times, these are things that make a person who they become. In many communities, there are life-altering liabilities that create more difficulties than necessary. There are no more or fewer difficulties in an impoverished community than upper-income communities.

For example, music is everywhere, and any race or age of a child may listen to negative music may lead them to random thinking, acting out, and practicing what they heard. If the music is negative, this may lead to the kid developing behavioral problems from what was heard in the music such as shootings, people dealing drugs, having unprotected sex, or fights, etc. On the other hand, if a child listens to positive music, this may lead to the child doing some good, such as giving back to their community, helping their peers and others. Putting an end to bullying, saying no to drugs. Certain propaganda such as television, videos, and other media have positive and negative effects on a child's mind. A child may walk to the corner store around their neighborhood and see one of the neighbors standing on the corner selling drugs, then they go and try doing the same things, or the child may see the same neighbor getting incarcerated by the police and decide they want to become a police officer instead. A child may see the man across the hall from him in his apartment building hitting his wife, so when that child becomes an adult, they avoid relationships.

> The only way to do great work is to love what you do. – Steve Jobs

Dad was Not There

In many households across the world there are only moms at home, so when a situation happens, the child must begin making plenty of decisions on their own, while plenty of times while the mom is off to work or her other job trying to make ends meet. Many times, the kids stay at home or are outside watching themselves, often with the oldest child watching the younger siblings. Indeed, this is not the case for every household. Let's get one thing straight: there are plenty of households that have a live-in dad as well. Dads are just as great as moms. You have many situations where the father is a single parent who must raise the children on his own. There is not a "one size fits all." In many other households there are no parents, and the children must raise themselves. No matter who a child has, whether it's the mom or dad or themselves, an idle mind is the worst thing for anybody to have, especially a child. A child or anybody with too much time on their hands is not good. If this problem occurs, there are things a person may be able to do, such as enrolling the child into an afterschool program. They say an idle mind is the devil's workshop. Some circumstances can't be changed like whether family, race, tax bracket or the city where you were born, but you can change how you face them and your approach to dealing yourself a different hand.

> We are really competing against ourselves. We have no control over how other people perform.
> Pete Cashmore

Saying No to Drugs

Sometimes in life, things happen we cannot control, things like family we grew up in, the race we were born, the people around us who do drugs. Whether it's our schools, around our neighborhood or in in our very own home. That's right, I said it. You heard it right: in our very own homes. Why it would be a great thing for us to think that our mothers, fathers, brother and sisters, aunts, uncles, friends, or co-workers can't be a drug addict. Why? Because they are human and just because that person is a person you may have respected or looked up to at some point in your life or your entire life, doesn't mean they are exempt from things like over-dosing. A home invasion due to other addicts looking for drugs, police raiding your home, one of your younger family members possibly finding a baggie lying around on the floor and over-dosing from playing with the contents of the bag or the whole family getting evicted due to the rent and all the other bills not getting paid, because the parent or parents kept prolonging the bills and using the money for drugs instead. Family or friend getting shot over the drug, selling all the valuables and out of the home or pawning all of one's items or belongings. Maybe or just maybe it's you who is having the problem with drugs. Even if you have an addiction, the first thing you must do is acknowledge there is a problem. You're then able to start working on the solution to your problem. You may be one of the many people who experience plenty of things above or like some of your friends who didn't get a chance to allow many of the things on that list to happen because some of them died on the spot, or if they didn't die, they sure wish they had because a young child in their family died from some drug that had been lying out or fell out of their pocket. Try to get help as soon as possible. If none of those reasons is good enough for a person to say no to drugs, let that child's life be the reason you change, even though you're sick and know how to hide things. Think back to when you were a kid, how you got into everything you weren't supposed to be in. You know the saying, what happens in the dark eventually come to light or would be found by a child in the light, then at that point everything will turn dark.

Think about this: how could you live with yourself if a child overdosed and died from something you already knew as a liability. Drugs are a huge liability: they cost you everything, everyone, anything, anyone. With drugs most of the time you pay with your life or freedom. No, and I repeat *no* escape comes from drugs. Either way you're still paying with your life.

> We cannot become what we need to be by remaining what we are. – Max DePree

What Happens in a Relationship Stays in the Relationship

What happens in Vegas stays in Vegas. What happens in a relationship stays within that relationship or should. When you and another person are in a relationship, good things happen. She surprises you; he brought me this or that. When things are going well, it is human nature to talk about the good things that happen to them. People always want those around them or even the world to know how well they are doing. Why else do we want the latest phone, new car etc.? Sometimes in life the same things that make us laugh make us cry. The same way your lover used to bless you by giving you gifts, they're now doing the same thing for someone else. Or you think they are, because you didn't ask them. You now jumped the gun. You finally had enough one day, so you called your parents to vent on how you felt about your spouse. You told everybody in your family what happened. Two weeks later your spouse come to you and tells you what really happened. You realize it was a misunderstanding at the bank, but now it's fixed. You told your family all of what you thought your spouse did. As time passed you got over what happened and you forgave your spouse, but your family will still and forever hate or not like that person because of that foolish misinformation you fed them.

> The secret of getting ahead is getting started.
> Mark Twain

Sunken Cost Effect

The sunken cost effect is the concept of using, losing more than and chasing after what was already lost or used instead of chalking the money up as lost. Don't chase after what is already lost or gone. Let's say you're at the casino and have been shooting dice all night. Not only have you been shooting dice, but you have been losing. So far you lost $200, but you don't stop; you keep on gambling, instead of just chalking up what you have already lost which is that $200. You stay there and keep on gambling and lose $3,000 chasing the $200.

The sunken cost effect comes in many forms, such as people, places, and things. Instead of just chalking up the smallest amount that was already lost, you keep digging yourself a deeper hole to get out. So, it's pretty much like this instead of putting something under your feet so you can have some support for when you try to reach up to again, you dig further down and traveling away from the top making it harder to get out of the situation you put yourself in. If it does not add value, get rid of it. Because if it's not holding you down, it's holding you up.

The sunken cost effect with people goes like this. A person might start off being an asset and then they turn into a liability. Even hanging around a close-minded person waiting for them to change and start giving good advice is a form of sunken cost effect, because you will lose more staying around than waiting for their never arriving transition.

> Don't follow the crowd, let the crowd follow you.
> Margaret Thatcher

Good Debt vs. Bad Debt

You have good debt and you have bad debt. What's the difference between the two? The difference is that good debt is used to make money, so you pretty much borrow money to make more money. Bad debt is when you owe money from borrowing money. Good debt is when you borrow money to make more money. Bad debt is when you spend the money you borrow and don't make anything; you only owe money.

Let's say that you go to your bank and borrow five thousand dollars. But you don't just borrow the $5,000, you spend it on stupid things/liability that are not going to bring any money or income in. You choose the difference between asset and liabilities, so you took the $5,000 and purchased three vending machines. After about two weeks of having the vending machines at your location you made $6,000 total from your $5,000 investment. You use the $5,000 debt you turned good because you spent the borrowed money to flip and make more money through receiving an ROI (return on investment). Now you know what good debt and bad debt is. Depending on how a person uses their debt, this will establish good or bad credit.

> Leadership is absolutely about inspiring action, but it is also about guarding against mis-action.
> Simon Sinek

How Children Can Start Earning Passive Income Streams

I know there are many people who've heard at some point in their life as a kid say, "I can't wait until I grow up so I can be rich." Well, those kids are in luck. How are you doing today? Fine, I hope. If there are any of you out there who aren't, you are now. Because today you are going to learn how to create your own financial fate. What or whose fate are we creating? The fate of our kids by teaching them how to manage money, flip, then re-invest what was already earned through various sources. Here we go.

If you, a kid or a teen or an adult for that matter have made it this far in life or in this book, know that you are still becoming. You have not fully arrived yet. I know a lot of youth out there feel like or question "so am I who I am going to be for the rest of my life? Absolutely not and that statement is false and definitely, the furthest from the truth.

If you're a kid or teen and have breath in your body and you're alive, you have a chance and you have a choice to use your chance wisely if you haven't made a big mistake as to where it would cost your life and freedom. Even if you're a kid or teen currently on death row, keep your head up as well because if you're alive you still have a chance; laws change every day. Things change and turn around all the time. Even though this book is for people of all walks of life, this chapter is formatted more for children and teens with a lot fewer restriction or no restrictions. So, let's venture back to your earning passive income streams.

Why are there various ways to earn income as an adult. There are certain restrictions that a kid or teen who is not incarcerated may also face. Age might be one of the main factors. There are ways to circumvent this problem. Let's say for example: A kid or teen mows someone's yard, cuts or styles someone's hair, does lashes, takes out a neighbor's trash, washes cars, paints houses, walks dogs, installs carpet to generate income. If you practice applying the intel from the previous chapters pertaining different types of income, many of you will notice many of these things like earned income. But hold on! You wouldn't be wrong, that's exactly what those things were: Jobs. In life as you become more and more responsible, you will begin to understand that sometimes you must take the proper small steps toward making the big things you want to manifest into reality. A great way for a kid or teen to start earning passive income is to save the money they gain from working a job from the earned income category. Whether they're getting paid by a real job where you pay taxes and receive a real paycheck, or the money is from getting paid under the table and off the record where you pay no taxes on what you earned, most of the under-the-table jobs you get paid in cash. No matter how you get paid, what you do with your check or money is very important. We all know what happens to people who get paid and don't save or invest. They live paycheck to paycheck. Most of these people will have nothing to show for but liabilities. On the other hand, you have the person who saved the money they earned from working a job. That person who saved their money for a rainy day or any day for that matter can now invest their money. A nice way to start some streams of passive income is to begin enrolling on Flippa.com. What you are buying is online digital real estate.

How Flippa.com works is simple. Let's say that a website cost $1,000 and it makes $400 monthly. You only pay this $1,000 onetime and one time only. What you're buying is domain names of websites that are already up and running. You can look on the site and it will tell you how much the site brings in monthly. There are different prices for different sites, so you must really look and do your research before you purchase anything. There are sites for all amounts.

> A wise person should have money in their head, but not in their heart. - Jonathan Swift

CA$H FLOW

Now you've made it to the point in this book where your financial IQ has matured. You now have the same choice and chance that you had at the start of the book, but the things that might have changed were your understanding and perception on money and how it works or should work for you. This bring us to cash flow and why you should start stockpiling cash cows so you could have streams of cash flowing in, even in the time of a pandemic, outbreak, or world catastrophic event where you won't be able to work because your city is shut down. You'll be prepared to take care and provide for yourself and family at the drop of a dime.

Start creating wealth and generational wealth by accumulating valuable assets and resources so you can pass it down from generation to generation along with your business associates and contacts. And speaking of assets and resources bouncing from generation to generation. We have Magic Bounce.

> Empty pockets never held anyone back. Only empty heads and empty hearts can do that.
> — Norman Vincent Peale

Magic Bounce

What's Magic Bounce? And why is it magical? Well, let me tell you that there is a very lucrative amount of money to be made in the rental moon bounce business. The magic is in how much you continue to make as time goes by. Depending on whether you get your moon bounce from, an online retailer site like Amazon.com or a manufacturer and wholesaler like Alibaba.com, no matter how or where, the number one goal is to rent them out to make huge profits.

Let's say that you buy a moon bounce for $1,500. Every time someone throws a party, they call you. Your party business also has snow cone machines, kettle corn, and cotton candy machines, and a DJ playing music. You might also have tables and chairs. For a rough estimate, you might charge around $500 for a basic package, with only just the moon bounce by itself for a few hours. For $700 gold package. you throw in kettle corn and snow cones and cotton candy machines, tables, and chairs for four hours. For a $900 platinum package, you get all the machines, tables, and chairs, DJ/music, and Arch. Remember there is no set price. When you are starting out you can adjust the price to bring in more clients. To get right to the bottom line. You paid $1,500 for the moon bounce and then you charge $500 to rent the moon bounce for four hours per party. After three parties at $500 a party, you've got your original $1,500 you initially invested. Now everything on top of your $1,500 is profit. Do the math: for example, 10 parties at the lease price are $5,000 depending on what party package your customers prefer. As is the same with any investment, don't forget to do your homework before spending any of your hard-earned cash.

Before you speak, listen. Before you write, think. Before you spend, earn. Before you invest, investigate. Before you criticize, wait. Before you pray, forgive. Before you quit, try. Before you retire, save. Before you die, give.

William A. Ward

How Vices Can Get out of Control

Speaking of hard-earned money, the way a person spends a lot of their money on vices, it can and may spiral out of control. When I mentioned vice, I'm talking about the excessive immoral indulgence of a person spending their income or money so loosely and reckless to the point of pleasure only. Vices like gambling, drugs, shopping, drinking, etc. things that feel good, where everything else takes a back seat. Then when the money runs low and the habit still exists or got larger, the person now results in ill-gotten gain, which is in most cases fast money. This thinking is that of liabilities. This thinking costs you many times; most of the times a person will result in the person getting killed or incarcerated. Because their habit will most likely cause the person to start running through their checks if they did have a job. So, they will resort to the fast pace quick buck because they're no longer able to keep employment. Some of the things on this list are not that bad; what makes something bad is when a person indulges and abuses things and doesn't use moderation. Too much or too little of anything can be bad.

> You can only become truly accomplished at something you love. Don't make money your goal. Instead, pursue the things you love doing, and then do them so well that people can't take their eyes off you. - Maya Angelou

How Fast Money Ends Slow Money

How does fast money become slow money? That's the thing fast money will always be, just: that fast. Here's how. When one earns fast money most of the time it's in the form of ill-gotten gain such as robbery, stealing or chopping cars, stolen goods, white collar scamming, numbers running, pimping, drug dealing, and trafficking. No matter, these are some of the main avenues a person may earn fast ill-gotten money. But wait a minute! What's the catch — because this sounds too good to be true. And, it is true, a person really can make money some of it if not all these ways. So, what's the catch? The catch is when the police catch you. Now you're in jail. Your fast money just turned slow. Why? Because many jails don't pay inmates at all. The prison labor camps there are covered up by the word "jobs." Just like the ones in foreign countries. They might have a four-million-dollar contract. But they pay out like $30,000 in all, to get that four-million-dollar job done. Or like $25 to $100/hour for your first year, it will probably take about five years for an inmate pay to reach $3 to $5/hour. Think about if you were to have had a legal job paying at least minimal wage. The working-class person making the consistent money, comes out on top over the person earning the fast ill-gotten money. One of the main things that fast money brings is jail and death. While the person is in jail, all of the people on the outside's relationships are affected.

> If you're saving, you're succeeding.
> Steve Burkholder

How Getting Locked-up Affects Relationships

When a person gets incarcerated, there are certain things that they go may through and experience. One of those things they experience is the distance and the strain that is put on a person's relationship, whether it's their relationship with family, lover, friends, co-workers, or neighbors —especially with their significant other. Depend on if they get a lot of time. Some things may vary. Because they are not able to be there with the person, out of sight out of mind can take place when it come to the mind of the free person. If it's a relationship with their lover, they might be strong and stick around or leave the person that's in jail to find someone else. The thing that might affect a person incarcerated and their co-workers is that the person might not have their job or position at work when they are released. The incarcerated person's relationship with the kids many times get affected, because if that person winds up getting a lot of time, their kids will grow up without them, as we covered in previous chapters of how children often become products of their environment due to negative choices made by their guardian or caretaker.

> Time well-spent results in more money to spend, more money to save, and more time to vacation.
> Zig Ziglar

Does the End Justify the Means?

By all means, is what a person may subconsciously or consciously tell themselves. Either way, this statement or thought is from the mindset of a person who says, "how can I afford that?" Most people soon after began to resort to their best way or means to accomplishing their goal. Most people might say it doesn't matter how you get to and interview just if you make it there and get the job. Hold up, wait a minute! How did you get there? I mean, how did you really get there? Let's recall the person early on in this book that rudely treated the man waiting for the parking space, disrespected, and knocked over the old lady in the building on the way to his job interview. This is the mentality of a person who lives by any means doctrine or set of principles. All times are not alike, and sometimes desperate times calls for desperate measures. That's why it's so important to enlighten yourself on different subjects and keep your analytic mind as sharp as possible. So, a person can move only in a righteous way, by doing straight legitimate business with the people they meet. Then spend their life to create wealth, then generational wealth and resources so the next generation can succeed while leaving a legacy for generations to come. This goes back to a chain, business, organization, family, any group with any goal for that matter is only strong or as weak as the weakest link.

Now that you understand that the #1 law of man or mankind is self-preservation, you now will realize that it's not just about you. It's about learning how to progress then teaching others like yourself to get out the snail race and stop living from paycheck to paycheck, paying bills, thinking, and living the lifestyle of a person that's a toxic struggling liability and consumer. But instead to live a great lifestyle of someone whose is healthy mentally, physically, spiritually and financially free. You only live once, so live for today and invest for the future of tomorrow. I guess sometimes the means do justify the end for the greater good of the whole. You now have time to change. Practice making the right choices because you don't have to be a product of your environment. By continually learning, building we uplift each other and impower ourselves through obtaining knowledge that's useful to give us better insight and ammunition to understand the battle that is taking place before our eyes. We will then be able and properly prepare and be ready on all planes and platforms. Because if you're alive and reading this then you know that people from all walks of life are still dealing with something that's as simple as acceptable or not among each other, such as racism, same-sex marriage, police reform, global warming, drug abuse, abortion, and gun violence.

As these things continue to go on around us, you still must keep in mind as you watch your surroundings. That no matter what, do 10% of the work and get 90% results. Have you ever rolled over in bed and had to get up and go to work? Imagine that you don't have to get out of bed. Why? Because you took all the proper steps. As you build your diverse portfolio, let your money make money by letting your money work for you. You've learned how to stop working for others and minding their business, but instead you realize that the more you tend to yourself, and your own business is less time you inevitably must spend working for anyone else. Don't forget that everything is a process and building wealth is a never-ending process, so always be mindful of the fact that a liability can arise at any given moment and do what they do. That's to make it difficult for you to get ahead in life; and to bring us to where we started. What life? Well, let me tell you. Life is what you make it! Just remember time waits for no-one. Keep in mind that knowledge is power, and power is resources. The Master power is resourceful and resources help you succeed. Everything is not going to be easy. If you fall, get back up brush yourself off. Take notes when things are going well, but really takes notes when things are going bad, so you don't slip up twice. Then as you get into the habit of progression only then is when you began to build your foundation brick by brick. Without your foundation you have no balance. You must be accountable for your life. If other people can move forward in life, why can't you show up and get the job done. We are the authors of our own destiny. If you don't like the narrative of your story, you can create a different one at any time. Remember time is the only thing that you really have in this world that counts down with each breath.

Health is wealth and vice versa. If you're stinking rich but your health is bad, what do you think is next? If your health is not on track, you're only going to spend that money on your funeral. You must be fit for survival mode, put yourself in the best positions in life — mental, physical, social, and financial — to better your chances at helping your family, business and race succeed.

Thank you for taking the time out to read this book!

Resource List of Inspirational Books

"Rich Dad Poor Dad" - by Robert T. Kiyosaki

"Think and Grow Rich" - by Napoleon Hill

"Message to the People" - by Marcus Garvey

"Mindset. Moves. Momentum." – by Julia Royston

"The Art of War" – by Sun Tzu

"The 48 Laws at Power" - by Robert Greene

"The Compound Effect" - by Darren Hardy

"The Financial Statement" - by Thomas Ittelson

"How to Be a Capitalist Without any Capital" - by Nathan Latka

"The Master Key System" by Charles F. Haanel

"Hustle Harder, Hustle Smarter" - by Curtis "50 Cent" Jackson

"How to Win Friends and Influence People" - by Dale Carnegie

"The Law of Success" - by Napoleon Hill

Thank you again for taking the time out to read this book!

To purchase more copies in English, scan the following QR Code

www.ingramcontent.com/pod-product-compliance
Lightning Source LLC
Chambersburg PA
CBHW050826160426
43192CB00010B/1918